T0208300

SCRIBE OF RIGHTEOUSNESS

God Almighty

authorHOUSE®

AuthorHouse™ UK Ltd.
500 Avebury Boulevard
Central Milton Keynes, MK9 2BE
www.authorhouse.co.uk
Phone: 08001974150

First published by AuthorHouse   7/18/2011

ISBN: 978-1-4567-7770-8

ACKNOWLEDGEMENTS.

Firstly, i will like to give thanks to the Author of all authors, GOD, the creator of heaven and earth, i say thank you LORD. Secondly, to the company that published my first and this book, the authorhouse and their team, i say thank you. Thirdly, my blood brother Jimi, who helped me to design the cover of my first and this book, i say thank you. PSALM 68-11. The LORD gave the word, great was the company of those that published it.

A WORD FROM GOD, TO THE READER.

MATTHEW 13-52.

Then said he unto them, therefore every scribe, which is instructed unto the kingdom of heaven, is like unto a man that is an householder, which bringeth forth out of his treasure things new and old.

THE KINGDOM OF GOD, IS LIKE OWNING A BUSINESS.

The kingdom of GOD, is like a people, that cried to GOD, regarding owning a business or portion in life, for themselves and the next generation after them. The Almighty GOD, sent one a saviour, to go and fulfil their prayers.

The saviour came, prepared the way, by creating a business for that set of people. But when the business was up and running, the saviour came and told the people to come and buy. But the same set of people, that petitioned their GOD for that prayer, despised their saviour and went their own way.

Unknown to them, that, that saviour, that was despised has the key of David, the chief corner stone, who open and shut at his will. And because they despised that one, they failed to see, what they should have seen.

This is what the kingdom of GOD is like.

(Written, by GOD Almighty, through me on the 15/12/2007)+.

THE LORD'S, ANSWER TO EGYPT.

The city of habitation meaning persistence, endurance and preserverance.

And he led them forth by the right way, that they might go to the city of habitation. And there he maketh them hungry to dwell, that they may prepare, a city of habitation. LORD give me help from trouble, for vain is the help of man. It is good that you afflicted me, LORD, that i might dwell in the city of habitation. Let my heart be sound in thy statutes, that i be not ashamed, and dwell in the city of habitation, so that my race and seed, that came out of my loin, will inherit the city of habitation .

LORD of all spirits, your voice will i hear. Another gods voice, will i not hear, you said that my sheep knows my voice. The voice of the god of canaan, will i not hear. The voice of the god of this world, will i not hear, the voice of the god of Egypt, will i not hear, they are not the one, who laid the foundation, of the city of habitation. The GOD of the righteous, will i hear, you LORD, laid the foundation of the city of habitation. The GOD of Abel the righteous, the GOD of seth, the GOD of Enoch the righteous, the GOD of Noah, the GOD of Abraham, Isaac and Jacob, the GOD of Melchizedek, the GOD of Job, the GOD of David, and myself, the GOD that i came to know.

LORD of all spirits, remember you are the GOD of ham, before ham sinned. You laid the foundation of ham, the city of habitation. I know full well that ham sinned, and his seed against you and served the idols, which were a snare unto them. They sacrificed their sons and daughters, whom they sacrificed unto idols, and the land of ham was polluted with blood. They also sacrificed, their sons and daughters unto the devil. Thus ham was defilled with their own works, and went a whoring, with their own invention. Therefore your wrath LORD, was kindled against your people, the people of ham, in so much that you aborred your people. Remember LORD, of old, that the devil, is not the LORD of ham, but you are the LORD, over the people of ham. Have mercy over the people of ham, and return over your habitation, for the people of ham, welcome you back with open hands and a pure heart.

Of a truth, LORD, a burden is upon Egypt, the son of ham. And the Egyptian will be set against an Egyptian, brother against brother, neighbour against neighbour, city against city, kingdom against kingdom, and the spirit of Egypt will fail, and in the midst destroy their counsel. Therefore they shall seek to the idols, and to the chamers, and to them that have familar spirits, and to the wizards. And the Egyptian, will be given over unto a cruel lord, and a fierce king, shall rule over them, saith the LORD the LORD of host.

LORD, the son of ham, pharoah an Egyptian boasted against you, surely your word remains true, and shall stand.

Surely the princes of zoan are fools, the counsel of the wise counsellers of pharoah is become brutish, how say ye unto pharoah, i am the son of the wise, the son of ancient kings? where are they? where are thy wise men? and let them tell thee now and let them know what the GOD of host, hast purposed upon Egypt, (the people and the land of ham). The prince of zoan are become fools, the prince of noph are deceived they have also seduce Egypt (the land of ham and his people). Even they that are stay of the tribes thereof. The LORD hath mingled a perverse spirit, in the midst thereof and they have caused Egypt to err, in every work thereof as a drunken man staggereth in his vomit never shall there be any work for Egypt, which the head or tail branch or rush may do.

Of old LORD, great things you've done for ham and the land of ham, please pardon our iniquities.

LORD of all spirits, our saviour at one time was resident in the land of ham, christ in Egypt.

Moses a man of GOD, who knew you face to face was resident in the land of ham, in Egypt.

Moses wife, was a daughter of ham zipporah.

Joseph one of the sons of Jacob, was sold into the land of ham, and also became prime minister of the land of ham. Joseph wife, was a daughter of ham an Egyptian.

LORD your paradise, was in the land of ham, the garden of eden also LORD remember that you said, that great things will come out of the land of ham, let it be so.

The Queen of Sheba, came from the land of ham, the Queen of the south, to hear the wisdom that you've put in the mouth of a great and wise king, king Solomon of Israel.

Solomon's mother, the wife of king David was a daughter of ham.

Blessed is the son of ham, whom thou choosest and causest to approach unto thee, that he may dwell in the courts and shall be satisfied with the goodness of thy house, even of thy Holy temple the city of habitation. For prince, shall come out of the land of ham, and ham shall soon stretch out her hands unto the LORD of all spirits.

In that day shall there be an altar, to the LORD, in the midst of the land of Egypt, and a pillar at the border thereof to the LORD and it shall be for a sign and for a witness unto the LORD of host, in the land of Egypt for they shall cry unto the LORD because of the oppressor and he shall send them a saviour, and a great one, and he shall deliver them.

And the LORD shall be known in Egypt, and the Egyptian shall know the LORD, in that day and shall do sacrifice and oblation. Yea they shall vow a vow, unto the LORD and perform it. And the LORD shall smite Egypt, he shall smite and heal it, and they shall return even to the LORD and he shall be entreated of them, and shall heal them. The LORD of host shall bless, saying blessed Egypt my people (the land and the people of ham.)

Note.

One of the curses, the creator put on Egypt, he said, never shall there be any work for Egypt, which the head or tail, branch or rush may do. Which is a curse of idleness, to reverse this curse on Egypt, Egypt must start worshipping the true GOD. In a way what GOD did, was to sign Egypt with the cross of christ.

Egypt the people of the LORD.

Assyria the work of the LORD'S hand.

Israel the inheritance of the LORD.

The city of habitation is the new jerusalem or paradise.

(Written, by GOD Almighty, through me on the 14/12/2007)+.

O MIGHTY MAN, TEACHING ERROR.

O mighty man, you go across the sea to win souls, for the LORD and saviour, as the LORD our GOD said. But when you see that they are in the house of the LORD, doing the will of GOD, you put so much burden on them that they do worst than before.

O mighty man, just because you do not want to lost control, of your false bishopric, woe unto you, and your agents. O mighty man, who leads GOD'S people astray by teaching error.

O mighty man, you tell the flocks what they want to hear, that way they do not fulfil their destiny in life, because you've given them false hope. As a flock in the house of GOD, they should overcome. But because of what you tell them, they are not overcoming at all. Woe unto you, o mighty man, full of error.

(Written, by GOD Almighty, through me on the 15/12/2007)+.

THE THRONE OF GOD.

Solomon the king of Israel, replicated, the throne of the kingdom of GOD, in heaven on earth. To my understanding, i know that the throne of GOD Almighty, is placed on the seventh heaven. Also to my understanding, the Holy bible talked about the first, second heaven and so on.

In 1 Kings 10:18-20, Solomon made a plan of the kingdom of GOD, GOD's throne, in heaven on earth.

King Solomon made a great throne of ivory, and over laid it with the very best gold.

The throne had six steps, and the top of the throne was round behind, and there were stays, on either side on the place of the seat, and two lions stood beside the stays.

Twelve lions stood there on the one side, and the other upon the six steps. There was not the like made in any kingdom.

In the kingdom of GOD, the seventh heaven is where the throne of GOD is located.

In the kingdom of GOD, the six steps are the six heavens.

The two lions, on opposite sides, are the two anointed one's that stay by GOD.

The twelve lions, each one, of the head of the tribe of Israel, judging their tribe. Six on the right side, and six on the left side, like sitting round table in a board room meeting, looking up to the king of kings, or judge of all judges. That's why there was not the like, made in any kingdom. I hereby draw a visual plan

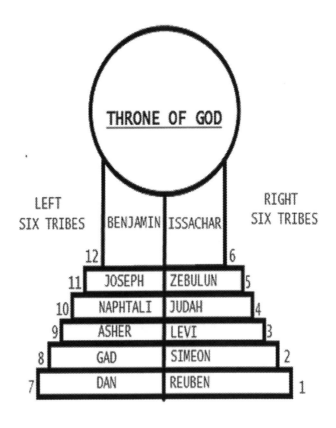

(Written, by GOD Almighty, through me on the 17/12/2007)+.

SET THINE HOUSE IN ORDER.

O mighty GOD, the LORD of all spirits, that dwells between the cherubims. You are GOD, above the heavens and the earth.

The enemy said, to me, set thine house in order, after i have destroyed, the gathering of the evil one, so that i could depart this earth. But while i was about to do it, the LORD of all spirits, replied to me, i haven't told you so, so why set thine house in order.

I told my LORD and my GOD, the creator of all spirits, that i have lived, every day of my life set in order. Daily will i look up to you in heaven, waiting for your second return, on earth. For the sons and daughters, the true sons and daughters of GOD, seek your second return. So that the evil one, will be abase forever. My house is set in order, daily LORD, LORD of all spirits, for your second return.

(Written, by GOD Almighty, through me on the 19/12/2007)+.

NEW YEAR RESOLUTION.

The best way to make and stay, with a new year resolution. Let's suppose you have ten bad habits, that you want to see a change, in your life. What you have to do, is take one bad habit, work on it daily until you see a change, for a year and overcome that bad habit. Then go on to the next one, the next bad habit, until you finish the ten bad habits.

The worst thing one could do, is make a new year resolution at the start of the year, because it's very difficult to keep at it. The best or great thing, to do is start right now, doing what you want done in the new year. Every new day, is a new year, so start right now. You can use this key, in any part of your life i.e your prayer life, and much more.

A great revelation given to me. (Written, by GOD Almighty, through me on the 30/12/2007)+.

LORD, WHAT A LIFE OF DISCOURAGEMENT.

LORD, what a life that all his neighbours are mindful of him, to see his end. On a beautiful day, i saw a lady that i knew going the same way, i was going. I pulled up, my brother gave up his seat, for that lady. The first thing, that came out of her mouth, was discouragement towards me.

I got to the shop, started trading for the day, the first customer, a so called pastor, man of god, pastoring his own church, the son of beliar, a false prophet, an hire servant came into the shop, the first thing, that came out of his mouth, was discouragement towards me.

My next door neighbour, in business, came into the shop, the first thing, that came out of her mouth, was discouragement towards me.

The post man, likewise, who came to deliver the mail, the first thing, that came out of his mouth, was discouragement towards me.

I went for a walk, i took a book to read, i saw an unknown man, sending abuse towards me, a day full of discouragement towards me.

LORD, what a life of discouragement? But my LORD, you are great, you gave me a book and a chapter to read, to regain my courage. The book that you gave me, is Job: 22. I read, and got my courage back, when i read verse 21 of chapter 22 of the book of Job .Verse 21 say's

21. Acquaint, now thyself with him, and be at peace, thereby good shall come unto thee.

22. Receive, i pray thee, the law from his mouth, and lay up his words in thine heart.

23. If thou return, to the Almighty, thou shalt be built up, thou shalt put away iniquity far from thy tabernacle.

25. The Almighty, shalt be thy defence, and thou shalt have plenty of silver.

26. For then shalt thou have thy delight, in the Almighty, and shalt lift up thy face unto GOD.

27. Thou shalt make thy prayers, unto him, and he shall hear thee, and thou shalt pay thy vows.

28. Thou shalt also decree a thing, and it shall be established, unto thee, and the light shall shine upon thy ways.

29. When men, are cast down, then thou shalt say there is lifting up, and he shall save the humble person.

30. He shall deliver the island, of the innocent, and it is delivered, by the pureness of thine hands.

Just remember this in the same book of Job 8: 19, 20, 21, 22.

19. Behold this is the joy, of his way, and out of the earth shall others grow.

20. Behold, GOD will not cast away a perfect man, neither will he help the evil doers.

21. Till he fill thy mouth, with laughing, and thy lips with rejoicing.

22. They that hate thee, shall be clothed with shame, and the dwelling place, of the wicked shall come to nought.

The next day, the potent GOD, delivered me from all my enemies, and the latter verse came to pass .

(Written, by GOD Almighty, through me on the 26/03/2008)+.

WHY BOASTEST.

O mighty man, why boastest, thou thyself in mischief. You are in a position of power, to influence the people of GOD, to do the right thing. But you let the devil, rule over you. You said, just because you are black, dosen't mean, you should come and support my business. What type of message, are you giving out to GOD'S people, not to love and go into another black business. Don't you know, that my business, is of GOD Almighty, and it's for the next generation, to come and be partakers of the righteous.

Did you not read, in the holy bible, what David said in the 52 psalm, while he was still living. When Doeg the edomite, came and told saul, the king of Israel, and said unto him, David is come to the house of Ahimelech.

As, the Almighty GOD, gave David the victory, over saul and doeg the edomite, likewise, my GOD will give me victory, over you and put you to shame. Let me put it again into your memory.

1. Why boastest thou thyself in mischief o mighty man? the goodness of GOD endureth continually.

14

2. Thy tongue deviseth mischief, like a sharp razor working deceitfully.

3. Thou lovest evil, more than good, and lying rather than to speak righteousness. Selah.

4. Thou lovest all devouring words, o thou deceitful tongue.

5. GOD shall likewise destroy thee forever, he shall take thee away, and place thee out of thy dwelling place, and root thee out of the land of the living. Selah.

6. The righteous also shall see, and fear, and shall laugh at him.

7. Lo, this is the man that made not GOD is strength, but trusted in the abundance of his riches and strengthened himself in his wickedness.

8. But i am like a green olive tree in the house of GOD. I trust in the mercy of GOD, forever and ever.

9. I will praise thee forever because thou hast done it and i will wait on thy name, for it is good before thy saints.

(Written, by GOD Almighty, through me on the 7/04/2008)+.

MAN OF SORROW.

If you are a man of sorrow, born of sorrow, live in sorrow, be a man who is acquainted with sorrow, you will alway's overcome the enemy, and be able to manage the affairs of life better. Life will be sweet to you because after sorrow, comes joy. But if you are a man acquainted with wealth, pleasure, enjoyment making merry, always going to the house of enjoyment, i.e churches where the pastor or overseer, makes you feel good, and not make you feel GOD, life will be unfair to you because after joy comes sorrow.

The ancient prophets, of old, in the old and new testaments, never pray for deliverance from man. They prefer to go through, whatever GOD brings their way. O LORD, i know that the way of man is not in himself, it is not in man that walketh to direct his steps. GOD himself gives deliverance, at his will. Deliverance to GOD means, that you want to die and come home to him, your maker. The prophets of old refuse the deliverance, from man but accepts the deliverance from GOD.

Some of the prophets who knew about this key are as follows. Abel the righteous, was one of them. Enoch the righteous, the seventh, from Adam was one of them. Noah was one of them, the tenth, from Adam. Abraham, Isaac, and Jacob were one of them. Moses was one of them. David the king of Israel, was one of them. Isaiah the prophet, was one of them. Jeremiah, Ezekiel the prophets, were one of them. Daniel and the three hebrews, were one of them. Job the righteous, was one of them. Paul was one of them. And how can i forget my LORD and my GOD Jesus Christ, the fountain of living water, was the ultimate one. So you see being a man, acquainted with sorrow, has alot of pluses and no minuses. Solomon a great and a wise king, the wisest man of his time, learnt this key the hard way, when he said, that it's better to dwell in the house of sorrow, than to be in the house of joy. Acquainted with sorrow, make you acquainted with the fountain of living water, who is life and life is GOD.

(Written ,by GOD Almighty, through me on the 30/05/2008)+.

GOD'S LOVE OR JAH LOVE.

O pastors, o priests, o prophets, o leaders, o kings, o prince, this is directed mainly to the pastors, priests, and prophets in the house of GOD, i.e in churches. The LORD, GOD Almighty, has seen a great evil, in the churches of today. You come to the house of GOD, use the people of GOD, to get a name. When the LORD, blesses you, you forget the house and the people of GOD, because you've gotten a name, which is vain in the eyes of the Almighty. Using your vainty name, to milk the people of GOD.

Some of you pastors, priests and prophets instead of you to look towards the flock, and do the work entrusted to you by GOD(JAH) with all of your heart. You do not preach, what is right to the flock, because GOD'S love or JAH love is not in you, but the love of vainty. Your wrong preaching, makes the people of GOD (JAH) to go astray, by scattering them abroad looking for what is vain like yourself. Surely you are not of GOD(JAH) because the love of GOD(JAH) is not in you, you speak of the world, and the world heareth you.

We the flock, are of GOD(JAH) hereby the spirit of error, is not in us. The people of GOD(JAH) come into the house of GOD(JAH) to give their tithes, and offering's to the house of GOD(JAH) with all of their hearts, and you wicked pastors, prophets and priest, so called in the house of GOD blocked them. The people from moving forward with their lives. If they put in your mouth or not, you rise up war against them, because of your own laws which you implement in the house of GOD(JAH). This is evil, and GOD(JAH) will deliver the righteous, out of your wicked hands and put you to shame.

I give you an example, i ran my own business, i pay my tithes to the house of GOD(JAH) in which i worship, and the people of that church will not come nor the pastor, priest, prophet come into my business. The pastor of that house, said that just because he is black, like myself doesn't mean that he should patronized my business. But what the same pastor forgets, is that my business is where i am able to pay my tithes, to the house in which i worship. This is a very great evil, that the eye's of GOD(JAH) has seen in the churches of today. When pastors preach messages like this, you put error into the flock and make them go after vainty like yourselves.

In 1 John chapter 4:6-21, but let me focus, on verse 20 and 21 of the same chapter. If a man say's i love GOD(JAH) and hateth is brother, he is a liar, for he that loveth not his brother whom he hath seen, how can he love GOD(JAH) whom he hath not seen? And this commandment, have we from him, that he who loveth GOD(JAH) loves his brother also.

So the remedy, of the whole matter is love, not just any love but GOD love (JAHlove) that we should love one another, pastors, priest, and prophets should first of all support or patronize the people of the house of GOD, and the people of the house of GOD should support one anothers business. Let the pastors preach, right things to the flock and not wrong things to the flock, whereby putting the people of the house of GOD(JAH) into error. Remember GOD love or JAH love is the greatest, commandment of all, nothing should be taught because of our own selfish gain.

NOTE: JAH is the short form for JEHOVAH in psalm 68:4.

(Written, by GOD Almighty, through me on the 19/05/2008)+.

THE KINGDOM OF GOD, IS LIKE BUILDING A HOUSE.

The kingdom of GOD, is like unto a man building a house. The man was given the grace, to build a house. But the grace GOD gave him, was to lay the foundation of the house, and not to build the whole house. This is the father.

His son, that came out of his own loin. GOD gave him the grace, to build the house to roofing level, and not to roof it. This is the son.

His son, that came out of his own loin. GOD gave him the grace, to roof, the house and not to inhabit it. This is the grandson.

His son, that came out of his own loin. GOD gave him the grace, not to roof, not to build the house, not to lay the foundation, but to inhabit the house, to occupy. This is the great grandson.

So you see, the kingdom of GOD, is like the completion of a house, with every generation that comes into the world, building into that kingdom.

(Written, by GOD Almighty, through me on the 1/07/2008)+.

BOOK OF LIFE (A SONG).

In the beginning, my LORD and my GOD, created the heavens and the earth. On the sixth day, he created man. Almighty GOD, created man, whom you loved like your own son. Man was created in your image, by you of course.

I loved you, LORD, since that day. From that day, i promised you, that i will love you, until the day that i die. GOD, you are my answer, i say that i will love you, till the day that i die. All i asked from you, is that you put me, in the book of life. The book of life, is where i want to be, so that i live, forever and ever. The book of life which never dies.

(Written, by GOD Almighty, through me on the 1/08/2008)+.

AM DETERMINED, TO WORSHIP AND SING PRAISE.

O LORD of all spirits, my mind is determined to worship you, and sing praises all of my days.

Though you afflict me, i am determined to worship and sing praises.

Though false prophets, gang up against me, i am determined to worship and sing praises, and serve you all of my days.

Though family members, and people of my race or people of the land, forsake and despised me, i will worship and sing praises unto you all of my days.

Though things, of the underworld, come against me, i am determined to worship and sing praises unto you all of my days.

Like Job the righteous, said, i will wait untill you redeem me.

NOTE: Underworld i.e Demonic activities.

(Written, by GOD Almighty, through me on the 11/08/2008)+.

FORCE THE DEVIL TO OBEY.

All the kings of the earth, shall praise thee, o LORD, when they hear, the word of thy mouth.

Though the LORD be high, yet hath he respect unto the lowly, but the proud he knoweth afar off.

Though i walk in the midst of trouble, thou will revive me, thou shalt stretch forth thine hand against the wrath of mine enemies and thy right hand shall save me.

The LORD, will perfect that which concerneth me, thy mercy, o LORD endureth forever, forsake not the work of thine own hand.

So therefore the devil, and his agents, his sons, daughters, his false prophets, i will come against to destroy totally out of the land of the living. I will force that disobedient spirit, to do the will of my living GOD, and his agents, sons, daughters including his false prophets likewise.

As a lion, crusheth a bone, in his mouth that was caught as a prey, so will i crush the disobedient spirits and his agents.

As a leoperd, killeth his prey, so will i destroy the devil and his agents.

As the cheetah, pursueth his prey and overtaketh it, so will i pursue the devil and his agents.

As a man, dominated the demonic spirits, when my LORD Jesus christ gave power to his disciples. And they returned and reported that even the demons, are subjected unto them. Likewise, do i to all the disobedient and foel spirits, forcing the devil and his agents to obey.

(Written, by GOD Almighty, through me on the 16/09/2008 could be used as a song or prayer. Added psalm 138 few verses from the beginning)+.

GAZA LAND OF ETHIOPIA.

And David said, unto Achish, if i have now found grace in thine eyes, let them give me a place in some town in the country, that i may dwell therefore, why should thy servant dwell in the royal city with thee?

Then Achish, gave him ziklag that day. Wherefore ziklag pertaineth unto the kings of judah unto this day. (1 samuel 27: 5-6).

Likewise, Solomon the son of David, King of Israel, gave gaza to the Queen of Ethiopia, as a gift for coming from the south to see him. And to hear his great wisdom, which the Almighty GOD gave him. Solomon told her all her hearts desire, and she received, that which women greatly desired.

In the book of acts 8:26-27

26. But the angel of the LORD said to Philip, rise and go towards the south, to the road that goes down from jerusalem to Gaza. This is a desert road.

27. And he rose and went. And behold an Ethiopian, a eunuch, a minister of Candace the queen of the Ethiopians, in change of all her treasure, had come to Jerusalem to worship.

Gaza is still a place, of importance to the people, of Ethiopia. It's a desert road, that will be used by them to go and worship, the LORD of all spirits, at Jerusalem for the second coming.

So therefore Gaza, a lands of Ethiopia, for an inheritance unto this day.

(Written, by GOD Almighty, through me on the 17/09/2008)+.

READY WRITER.

I came to this world, i found them asleep, (my race asleep) empty my people came into this world, not knowing that they must fulfil, before departing out of this world. Empty they leave, without doing a task. I will rather be poor, and let the whole world laugh at me, and i accomplished my GOD given task, and return to my LORD and GOD fully loaded than sit and do nothing.

O foolish people, don't you know that without accomplishing on the earth, one cannot dwell with the LORD of heaven and earth. Jesus christ said, nobody liveth to himself.

So my people, the whole idea is, though you came empty, into the world. One has to fulfil, one's GOD given task, before one departs out of this world.

Am a ready writer.

(Written, by GOD Almighty, through me on the 17/08/2008)+.

THE WORDS OF A BELOVED MOTHER, TO HER SON.

What my mum, told me.

She would say, my name three times. She would say, how many times, did i called your name? And i will answer my mother, you called my name three times.

She would say, remember the son of whom you are. Remember that we do not have any helper, but GOD. Remember that i am the only parent, you have.

As a mother, i will like to talk to you and put some words of advice your way, my son of my womb. Do not do business with other people, except with your beloved brother.

She would say to me, do not sell any of my belongings i.e houses, lands, property, businesses, used them to make more money between yourself and your brother.

She would say to me, find yourself a good wife. Who is also an helper, and do not let a woman used you like a cleaning stick. Women do not use men for games, these she would say in her mother tongue.(yoruba)

She would say to me, be very friendly to your brother and sisters, even if they do you wrong. (love them regardless).

She would say to me, alway's help people, in need, for this is from the Almighty GOD.

And her prayers, would go some what like these, i pray that i train my children, to the point that they are not afraid.

I pray that my children, will find helpers in life. I remember one day in her room playing ludo, the game with her, and she tried to give me a word of advice. And for some reason, i did not agree with her. She said something in yoruba, that say's i will not bother myself in your matter again. But had it been that i understood that saying, i would have listen to her and taken her advice. Not long after she died, and all the advice and saying came to me. She would say to me, remember the son of whom you are. She would called my name, don't you know who and what you are. These are words that my beloved mother, gave me while she was still alive, and i have kept them ever since. To my beloved mother, how i wish that you are around, i miss you.

(Written, by me, on the 18/08/2008)+.

MOTE OUT OF YOUR EYE,BEAM OUT OF MY EYE.

MATTHEW 7:3-5.

And why beholdest thou the mote that is in thy brother's eye, but considerest not the beam that is in thine own eye?

Or how wilt thou say to thy brother, let me pull out the mole out of thine eye, and behold a beam is in thine own eye?

Thou hypocrite, first cast out the beam out of thine own eye, and then shalt thou see clearly to cast out the mote out of thine brother's eye.

You cannot give to your brother, what you do not have. Jesus christ first of all cast out the mote out of his own eye, (dust) and was able to cast out the beam out of his brother's eye. So you see, a man, who could not cast out the devil or demons from himself, could not cast it out from another man, or from the members of the flock. If you haven't being there, you could not tell someone, how to get there. That is, who or what, an hyprocrite is. An hyprocrite, will first cast out the mote out of his brother's eye, before he cast out the beam out of his own eye, causing more problems than good. When you serve an impotent god, you make the life of the flock difficult. But GOD's name is potent.

(Written, by GOD Almighty, through me on the 30/10/2008)+.

A WOMAN CANNOT BE THE HEAD,
OF THE CHURCH.

In the beginning, in the kingdom of GOD, GOD is the head of all the spiritual beings. GOD'S wife is the Holy spirit, and the son of that marriage is christ. These three, are one to GOD the father. While in the physical realm, GOD Almighty reproduce what is in heaven on earth. He created Adam, and from Adam came his wife Eve, and from that marriage came Abel.

These three, are one to GOD the father. GOD the father created Adam in his image, while Eve was created in the image of Adam. Adam was the only man ever who wasn't born from a woman, while Eve was the only woman ever that wasn't born from a woman. On that note GOD the father, made them equal, but because of sin, Eve lost that right and was subjected unto her husband.

Now the head of the church, is GOD the father. Christ married the church, his wife, and from that marriage came the righteous members, sons and daughters. These three, are one to GOD the father.

So you see, a woman cannot head the church, because the Holy spirit is female. And a female cannot marry a female, that would be an abomination in the house of GOD. That's why christ said, that he's coming back to a church without blemish. He's coming back to his wife, because he married the church. You might ask why i say that the Holy spirit is female it's because the Holy spirit is compare to the church in the kingdom of GOD. Christ goes to his church, as his wife while GOD goes to the Holy spirit, as his wife.

And the LORD shall be king over all the earth, in that day shall there be one LORD and his name one(Zechariah 14-9)

If you go to the old testament, in the book of Leviticus. GOD Almighty chose levi, to teach the law of his GOD, to the tribe of Israel, not a woman but a man Levi, the son of Jacob.

In the book of Malachi 2:4-7

And ye shall know that i have sent this commandment unto you, that my covenant might be with Levi, saith the LORD of host.

My covenant was with him of life and peace, and i gave them to him for the fear, where with he feared me, and was afraid before my name.

The law of truth was in his mouth, and iniquity was not found in his lips, he walked with me in peace and equity and did turn many away from iniquity.

For the priest lips, should keep knowledge and they should seek the law at his mouth, for he is the messenger of the LORD of host.

FOOTNOTE:

Act 18:24-28(Read)

Act 19:1-6

1 Corinthian 14:34-36

Ephasians 5:21-33 (Very important)

Ephasians 5:24

1 Timothy 2:11-15 (Very important)

Revelation 2:20-22 (Very important)

(Written, by GOD Almighty, through me on the 10/10/2008)+.

THE MONKEY THAT PRAYED, TO GOD, THAT HE WANTED TO BECOME AN HUMAN BEING.

This story was told to me and my sister, by our late dad, at the age of about six or seven years old . From that early age, this story stuck to me like glue. This story goes somewhat like this.

There was once a monkey, who prayed to GOD, the Father Almighty, that he wanted to become an human being. GOD, the Father Almighty, told the monkey, that he will make him a deal, but the monkey has to keep is own part of the deal which the monkey accepted.

This is how the deal goes, GOD, the Father Almighty, told the monkey, to stay in a dark cave for seven days and nights without seeing day light, and on each day some changes will be in his body part. And that if he obey's that small and simple instruction, on the seventh day that he will become fully man, and the monkey agreed. GOD, the Father Almighty, told the monkey, that if he should go out of the dark cave at any time that the deal is off.

Now this monkey has a friend, who is fully man, a good friend of his. So the first day, the monkey stayed in the dark cave and truly after that day and night, he noticed some changes in his body part, his tail reduced in length.

Also the second day, the monkey stayed in the dark cave, and also noticed some changes to his body like the first.

This went on the third, and likewise unto the sixth day. But on the sixth night of the sixth day, the monkey's best friend, who is fully man came to him. Now fully man, is a man that likes to enjoy life. I will say the high life, he like to enjoy life to the full, like people of our present day do. He held an high life party, all manner of musical instrutments playing, drinks and women in abundance to the full.

Now the monkey, could hear the music playing but could not go out of the dark cave. Because of the deal, he had with GOD, the Father Almighty, so he stayed in the cave.

Fully man noticed, that at the party someone was missing, his best friend the monkey. So he went in search for him, and found him in the dark cave sitting by himself. Fully man asked, the monkey why he was sitting in the dark by himself, when the party is on going that he should come and enjoy himself. The monkey, now narrated the story, of the deal he had with GOD, the Father Almighty, to fully man. Fully man, laughed the monkey to scorn, and adviced the monkey, on what to do.

The advice, of fully man, to the monkey is this, that since the party, was in the night on the sixth day of the sixth night. That he should come and enjoy himself, and while it is still dark, he should go back into the cave, and on the seventh day, he becomes fully man.

So fully man, gave this advice, to the monkey, and the monkey went to enjoy himself at the party, and while it was still dark, the monkey went back into the cave.

On the seventh day, the monkey was very very happy, that after one more night, he will become fully man. But on the seventh day of night, the monkey, got a very big shock of his life. Because nothing happen, he's broken the deal with GOD, the Father Almighty.

Monkey prayed, to GOD, the Father Almighty, regarding the deal. But GOD, the Father Almighty, who is every where, even in the dark told the monkey, that he did not keep his own part of the deal and therefore the deal is off.

Monkey told, GOD, the Father Almighty, that fully man his best friend beguile him. Fully man said, that monkey, has a choice to obey, GOD, the Father Almighty, or to obey fully man, the choice is your's.

Truely that's why we have a monkey, till date with a short tail, that's the monkey in question.

Though this story is short, and simple, it has one million wise advice in it. The first and most important of all, is obey GOD, the Father Almighty .

FOOTNOTE:

This story, was told to me and my sister, by our late dad. I suppose that it's a kingdom story, and was told to my fathers before me, and my earthly father told me. And i am putting it down for my sons and future generation to come. To help them to understand that, obeying GOD, is very important.

(Written, by GOD Almighty, through me on the 4/12/2008)+.

THE KINGDOM OF GOD, IS LIKE THE REVERSE IS TRUE.

The kingdom of GOD, is like a pregnant woman, who is in labour and her time is come to deliver the baby. Two things come into place, the woman prepare herself to push, while the baby position it's self to come out of the womb. The woman's hour has come.

Also the reverse is true, in entering the kingdom of GOD, tribulation, struggle, that's why my LORD and my GOD, said that we enter the kingdom of GOD, through much tribulation. Every prophets of the old and the new testament knew this, that's why they all went through tribulation, that GOD, handed to them, as examples for us to follow.

Nicodemus a pharisees asked Jesus an important question in John 3:1-3 but verse 4 says. Nicodemus saith unto him, how can a man be born when he is old? can he enter the second time unto his mother's womb, and be born.

Picture that in reality, how a fully grown man, will re-enter his mother's womb, how difficult it will be for that man. That's the same way, one has to enter the kingdom of GOD, with much struggle and tribulation, and if there was an easy way,

Jesus christ would have let us know before he departed from this world.

(Written, by GOD Almighty, through me on the 6/12/2008)+.

THE KINGDOM OF GOD, IS LIKE A WISE FATHER AND A WISE SON.

The kingdom of GOD, is like a wise father and a foolish son, or a foolish father and a wise son.

A wise mother and a foolish daughter, or a foolish mother and a wise daughter. I tell you of a truth, that the kingdom of GOD is like a wise father and a wise son.

When you understand this you enter the kingdom of your father.

(Written, by GOD Almighty, through me on the 17/12/2008)+.

JESUS SON OF GOD.

Jesus son of GOD.

Jesus son of GOD, let me in.

Jesus son of GOD.

Jesus son of GOD.

Jesus son of GOD, let me in.

(A song, written, by GOD Almighty, through me on the 17/12/2008. I sang this song, in the dream, that i had of my head)+.

PARABLE, OF THE HOUSE OF PRAYER.

As in the days, of my LORD and my GOD Jesus christ, when he came into the temple of GOD. (Mark 11:15-17) Luke 19:45-46, Matt 21-13.

15. And they came to Jerusalem, and Jesus went into the temple and began to cast out them that sold and bought in the temple, and overthrew the tables of the money changers and the seats of them that sold doves.

16. And would not suffer, that any man should carry any vessel through the temple.

17. And he taught, saying unto them, is it not written my house shall be called of all nations the house of prayer? but you have made it a den of thieves.

So it was in my own days, worldly people, and so called worldly pastors, who brought cars, clothes, foods, and changing of money into the temple of GOD. Instead of the temple of GOD, being the house of prayer, it's become a temple of thieves (money making business).

But even in the latter days, when you see these happen, know that the second coming of my LORD and my GOD is drawing nearer even more nearer than you think.

(Written, by GOD Almighty, through me on the 20/12/2008)+.

THE SECOND COMING.

As it was from the days of Adam, until the crucifixion of my LORD and my GOD Jesus christ. So shall it be, from the crucifixion of my LORD and my GOD, Jesus christ, until the second coming, of the son of man, from the south.

(Written, by GOD Almighty, through me on the 14/01/2009)+.

PARABLE OF TWO MASTERS (LOVE AND HATE).

One master is called love, who is GOD Almighty. The other master is called hate, who is the devil. But these two masters, wanted this one slave, who is an humble and chosen slave.

This humble slave, has got no rights, but the master called love gives him his due, even if he doesn't ask for it. The other master called hate, do not give this humble slave his due, even if he asked for it.

Now the master called love, who is GOD Almighty, sold this chosen and humble slave, to the other master called hate, to know who the chosen and humble slave love, as a test.

While the chosen and humble slave, went to live and work for the master called hate, who is the devil. He found things which hate did that was wrong, just like his nature is. He tried to correct hate, but hate will not have any of his correction. Hate has so many slaves, working for him, some good and some bad, but all do the things that hate do. But for the love, that the chosen and humble slave has, though he knew all these things, lest he put the master hate, and his workers to shame. He endure all these things, for the love he has in winning the hate master and his workers, to the side, of his GOD Almighty, who is called love.

So you see, i know what is happening, but because of love, lest i put you and your workers to shame.

(Written, by GOD Almighty, through me on the 19/01/2009)+.

WILL NOT SEE CORRUPTION.

As my LORD and my GOD said, that i will not see corruption, corruption means death. This is a prophecy to my life, and i have told my family members, wife, and children that if they do not see my body that they should not look for me. Because the LORD of all spirits, the creator of heaven and earth has sent his chariot of fire, from heaven to pick me up. That's my desire because Enoch and Elijah did not see corruption, (which means death) i also will like to be the third person, in my aeon, not to see death or corruption in Jesus mighty name.

(Written, by GOD Almighty, through me on the 20/01/2009)+.

ENEMY AND HIS HOST.

I lifted up my mind, to GOD Almighty, the LORD of all spirits. The enemy say's in his heart, when will he finish, that his days comes to an end. But the son of man say's, all my day's, i have lived it, in an uncertainty, with the faith that the LORD of all spirits, had given me. I will put all my enemies and his hosts to shame. The uncertainty, that i had was the way, i was able to destroy the enemy and his hosts.

(Written, by GOD Almighty, through me on the 2/02/2009)+.

RESOURCES, NOT FOR YOU.

O kings and queens.

O priests, pastors, prophets.

O oba's, igwe's, emir's, chief's.

O leaders.

O princes, princesses.

O prime ministers.

O governors, governesses.

O presidents, of the contient of the south, the resources of the south is not for you, and the members of your families. The wealth, that you hold and enjoy, is not for you and your wicked doing. It's for the people, of the south. And most importantly, for the son of man, when he comes to take his aboard in the south.

Remember the south, is where my LORD and my GOD come's down, and alway's come's down upon the earth. You will give an account, of how you use the wealth, of my LORD and my GOD when he come's. Look he is right on his way, and before you know what is happening he will appear to you like a thief in the night. Then your shame, would be seen by all, and you would be force off that throne you are sitting on.

Stop misusing the wealth, of the south for your own personal gain, for the woe's of the LORD is upon you.

(Written, by GOD Almighty, through me on the 13/02/2009)+.

PEN, OF THE RIGHTEOUS SCRIBE.

The pen, of the righteous scribe, is not in vain, o you people of the LORD.

(Written, by GOD Almighty, through me on the 4/05/2008)+.

DEMON AT MY BED.(HOW I PREVAIL OVER IT)

How my LORD and GOD, gave me victory over the demon, that came to attack me on my bed, while i was asleep in my house.

This demon came, first, and i did not know what it was, and i will explain to you my experience.

I was at home, asleep, all of a sudden, i felt someone sat at my bed, by my feet. I did not know what it was, the thing moved towards my legs, my loins, my chest, my shoulders and my neck and at last my head. Then it was very difficult, for me to move, my head or my body, very difficult for me to break out of it. Because the demon was holding or putting pressure on my head. The way i was able to break loose, was to cry or call on the name of Jesus christ, at that name all knees, must bow, the demon left and i went back to sleep.

Second experience, same thing happened, but on this occasion the LORD taught me, that when i feel the demon sit at my bed, then that's the time to rain down fire and brimestone on the demon, and pray to destroy it's works.

The third experience, the same thing happen, i felt the demon sat on my bed, beside my feet. I started to pray, and rain down fire and brimestone, and the demon left, and did not come back again that night, weeks, months, years, etc.

My LORD and my GOD, the LORD of all spirits, showed me a revelation in the book of Ezekiel 47:1-6 but especially verse 3-6 it's called the vision of holy waters. This is the same way, that the demon, that sat on my bed worked. If you understand that verse, you will conquer the enemy on every sides. This also applies to the battle of life, any battle.

When the demon is by your ankles, it's easy to pray and defect the demon or enemy.

When the demon is by your knee's again, it's easy to pray and defect the demon or enemy, but not as easy when it was by your ankles.

When the demon is by your loins, it's difficult, to put it to flight. Because it's got hold of half of your body, now one has to fight harder to be able to overcome that demon, that's why in Ezekiel 47:5-6 it say's,

After ward he measured a thousand, and it was a river that could not pass over, for the water's was risen, waters to swim in, a river that could not be pass over.

And he said unto me son of man, hast thou seen this? Then he brought me and cause me to return to the brink of the river.

So the way to prevail over the demon's or the enemy, is when you go out and meet it at the onset, before the demon or the enemy gain entry.

(Written, by GOD Almighty, through me on the 19/02/2007)+.

CRY OF A FOOL.

This wisdom, have i seen also under the sun, and it seem great unto me.

There was a little church, and a few members within it, and there came a great law maker against it, and besieged it, by his laws.

Now there was found in it a young wise man, and by his wisdom, which GOD gave him could deliver the church. Yet no one wanted to call upon that young wise man.

Then said, i wisdom, is better than the wealth, of that preacher. Nevertheless the young man's wisdom is despised, and his words are not heard.

The words of the young wise man, are heard in quite, more than the cry of him that ruleth among fools. The fool that ruleth among fools, call for a loud cry of deliverance, but no one is delivered.

(Written, by GOD Almighty, through me on the 19/02/2009)+.

EVIL SPIRIT FROM THE LORD.

O motivational leader.

O inspirational teacher, why are you so jealous of me, just because you do not have my GOD, which is not for sale. Behold GOD Almighty, despised not any if you do the things that he commanded.

If my LORD and my GOD, told you to say all what you said on the pulpit about me, then you are doing the work which my LORD and my GOD, told you to do. How can i fight, against my LORD and my GOD, the Great creator of all.

But if you took it upon yourself, to do that, then you know surely an evil spirit, from the LORD is troubling you.

(Written, by GOD Almighty, through me on the 24/02/2009)+.

THE RIGHT BROTHER.

The affliction of GOD Almighty is great, it's greater than all affliction. In the midst of it all, you remain my GOD.

LORD of all spirits, i will like to thank you for my brother, you gave to me. Though you make my life easier, by your laws and commandments, which is better than money.

Thank you LORD, for a brother, that you gave to me. If i have three wishes, one of them is for you, to place my brother in my life. Thanks LORD, for putting the right brother, in my life.

(Written, by GOD Almighty, through me a short song about my brother the right brother on the 27/02/2009)+.

YOUR LAWS EVER GOOD LORD.

LORD i remember when i lost my earthly father, at my youth. I told my earthly mother, to help me bring your laws, that's to say my earthly father's bible, which is your holy bible. When my earthly father died, the first thing, i did was to take hold of your holy laws, which i read from my youth.

Also LORD, when my earthly mother died, also i took the same holy bible or laws and i started to meditate on them like a man who's looking for a bride. Remember what solomon said, he who findeth a wife findeth a good thing and received favour from the LORD. LORD your laws are ever good, it's like finding a wife and from them i received favour from you, LORD. When my father and my mother forsook me, then you took me up, by teaching me your way's, LORD. Your laws ever good, LORD.

(Written, by GOD Almighty, through me about my experience when i lost my earthly parents on the 2/03/2009)+.

DELIVERANCE PRAYER.

O LORD my GOD, help me, in the midst of my enemies. Put all my foes, to shame knownly and unknownly,. Every one of them that wants to see, my hurt. Let whoever it may be that want to see my hurt, go backward like their god, the dog. That does everything from the back.

But with you LORD, there is deliverance always, that's why, i keep going forward in all things. Whom have i in heaven, but thee LORD? and none upon the earth, that i desire beside thee LORD.

(Written, by GOD Almighty, through me a short prayer on deliverance on the 5/03/2009)+.

(A WORD FROM GOD, TO THE READER OF THIS BOOK)

Have you understood all this? They said to him, Yes. And he said unto them, therefore every scribe (of righteousness) who has been trained for the kingdom of heaven is like an householder who brings out of his treasure what is new and what is old.

MATTHEW 13:51-52.

OTHER BOOKS BY THE SAME AUTHOR.

1. SIMPLE -ISBN 9781449040970.

Also visit www.MYGODALMIGHTY.COM

OR

WWW.Authorhouse.com

OR

WWW.Amazon.com

CONTENT LISTS +.

19. A woman cannot be the head, of the church.

20. The kingdom of GOD, is like the reverse is true.

21. The kingdom of GOD, is like a wise father and a wise son.

22. Jesus son of GOD (song).

23. Parable of the house of prayer.

24. Second coming.

25. Parable of two masters, love and hate.

26. Will not see corruption.

27. Resources not for you.

28. Enemy and his host.

29. Pen, of the righteous scribe.

30. Demon at my bed.

31. Cry of a fool.

32. Evil spirit from the LORD.

33. The right brother.

34. Your laws ever good.

35. Deliverance prayer.

WARNING.

To preserved, the contents of this book for future genenation, i pronounce a blessing and forgiveness. A blessing to those who do the commandment of GOD, that they may have right to the tree of life, and may enter through the gates unto the city. For the second coming of my LORD and my GOD Jesus Christ is sure.

And forgiveness to those who are without the gates, dogs, sorcerers, whoremongers, murderers, idolaters, and whosoever loveth and maketh a lie by omitting or subtracting the truth from this book.

The Grace of my LORD Jesus Christ be with you all who obey, now and until the second coming. Amen.

NOTE: The scribe of righteousness is a compilation of 35 books or text which the LORD of all spirits wrote through me. These texts are of great importance to this present generation and to the one to come. It's short but within, is an hidden manner, GOD'S mystery in christ, in whom are hid, all the teasure of wisdom and knowledge, in the image of our creator. For GOD is the original scribe of righteousness.